This book belongs to

.................................................................................................

Age ................................

I started this book on ................................................

Max is written by Myrna Stent
and illustrated by Roy Mitchell

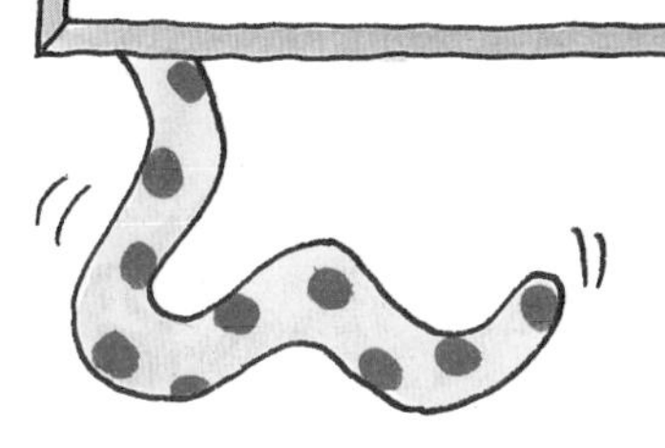

**To the teacher or parent:**

These books are a guide to a young pupil's first piano lessons. Unlike books 1 and 2 this volume does not include a set of bonus pieces at the end as the pupil should now be ready to widen their repertoire using music from other sources.

Further copies of the Max books and other Kevin Mayhew music available for use alongside this tutor are available from your local music shop. In case of difficulty, please contact the publisher direct:

The Sales Department
KEVIN MAYHEW LTD
Rattlesden
Bury St Edmunds
Suffolk IP30 0SZ

Phone 01449 737978
Fax 01449 737834

First published in Great Britain in 1995
by Kevin Mayhew Ltd



ISBN 0 86209 674 X
Catalogue No: 3611160



Music Editor: Anthea Smith
Music setting by Kevin Whomes
Printed and bound in Great Britain

Max the Musical Marvel is back
with another book of piano lessons.

I hope you have been practising hard –
I have been listening out for you.
along with all my friends.

Are you ready to start Book Three?

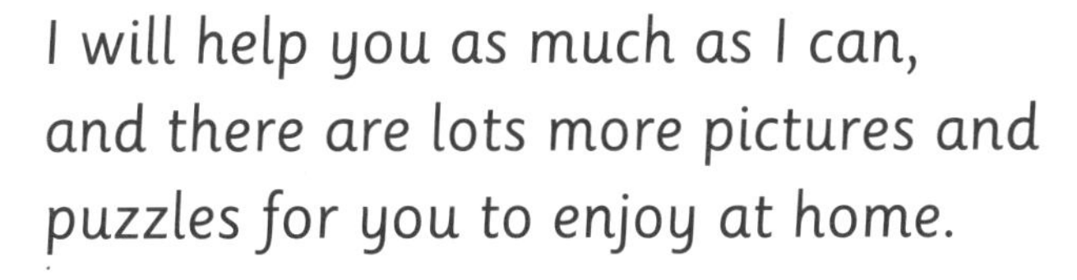

I will help you as much as I can,
and there are lots more pictures and
puzzles for you to enjoy at home.

When you finish this book,
your teacher will sign your

**MAX CERTIFICATE**

# Lesson 1

We will begin by playing the following scale exercises.

First, play with the right hand in the treble clef.

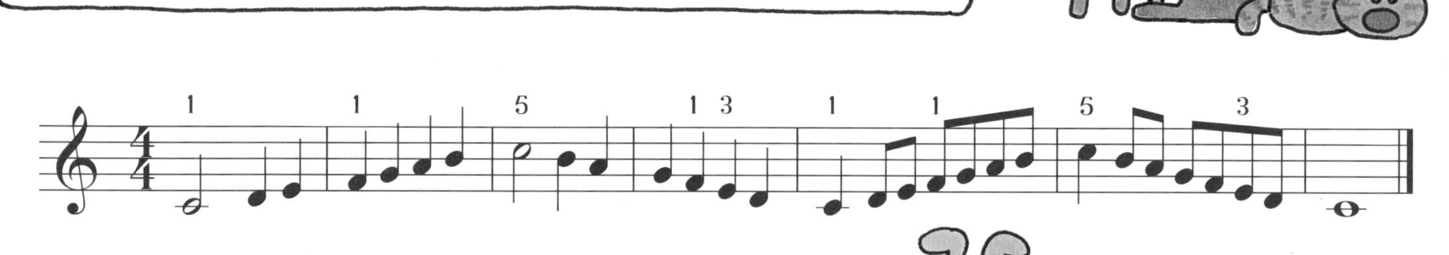

Now play with the left hand in the bass clef.

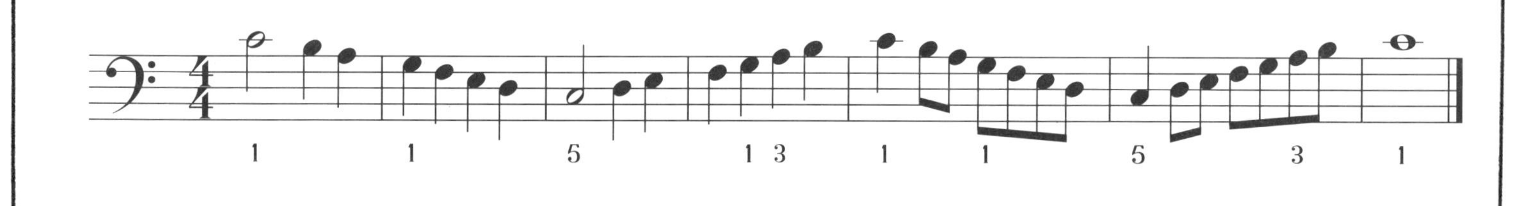

Try that just once more.

Can you play that hands together?
Each hand has the same note,
Middle C, with the thumb.

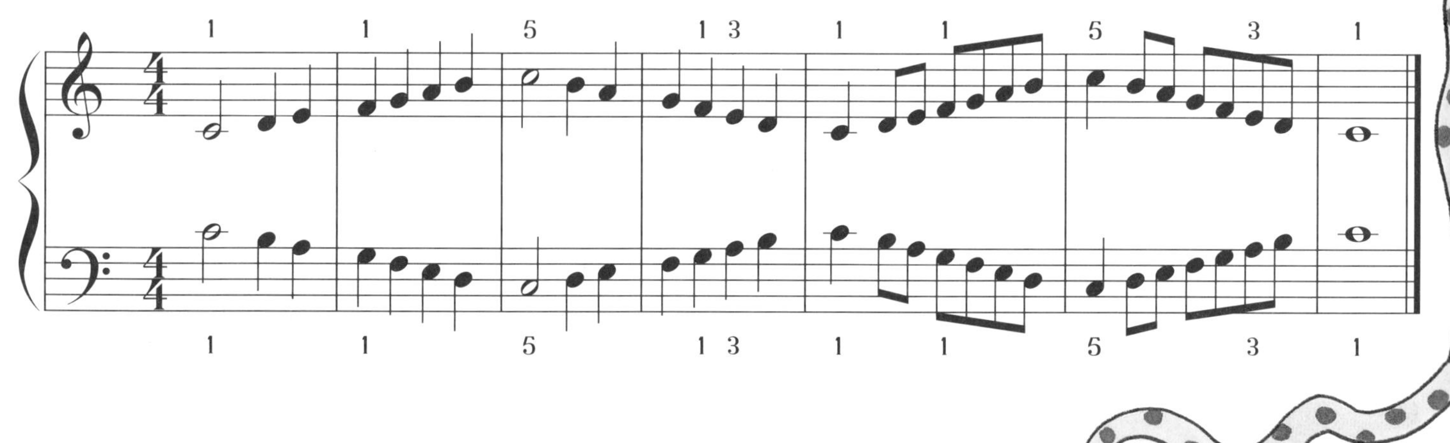

You have just played a scale in **contrary motion**.
What does that mean?
This means that the hands play in opposite directions.
I would like you to practise this scale exercise for next week and play it to me at the start of our next lesson.
Practise this next piece too.
Let's look through it to see if there is anything you do not understand.
CONTRARY MOTION
Moderato
Play smoothly
When you practise this piece, let each note glide on to the next, without any gaps.
We call this **legato**.
If you look at the back of this book, you will find a list of musical terms like this.

# Worksheet 1

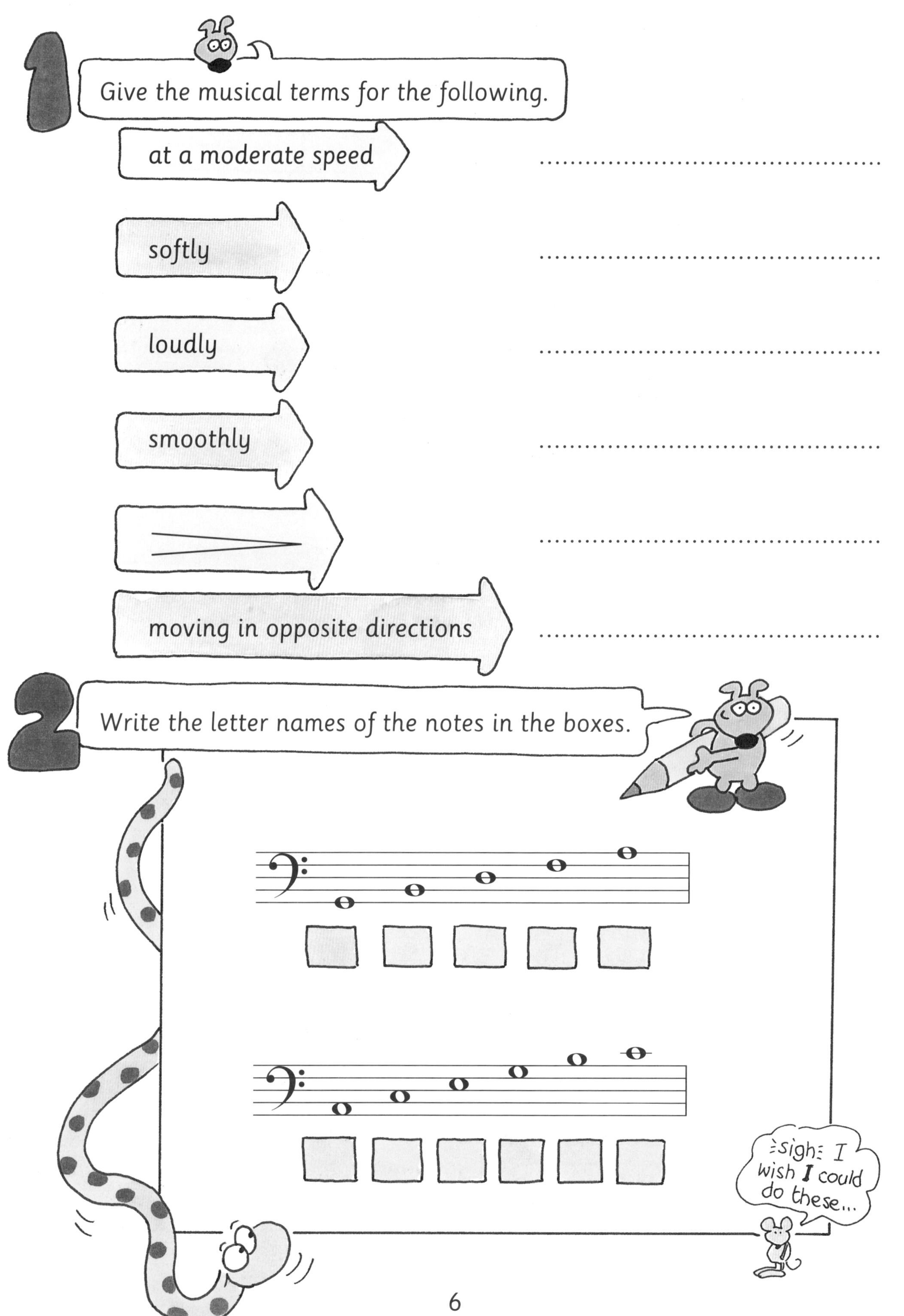
1
Give the musical terms for the following.
at a moderate speed ..............................................
softly ..............................................
loudly ..............................................
smoothly ..............................................
..............................................
moving in opposite directions ..............................................
2
Write the letter names of the notes in the boxes.
sigh I wish I could do these...

3
Write these notes two octaves higher in the treble clef.
SShhh!
4
Write in the names of these signs.
sigh I'm no good at writing...
T
S

Lesson 2
First of all today we'll play your scale in **contrary motion**.
Now play the piece you have practised.
Moderato
legato
CONTRARY MOTION
p
f
p
What does contrary motion mean?
Can you remember what it means, Sid?
Yes- it means your hands play in opposite directions!

Look at the next scale.
Make sure you look at the clef sign
so that you use the correct hand.
Er... I think that means use the left hand...
5 1 3 3 1 5
Did you recognise it?
Yes, it is a C major scale.
Now play it with the right hand only
starting on Middle C.
1 3 1 1 3 1
Watch your teacher play
this scale hands together.
Look carefully.
1 3 1 1 3 1
5 1 3 3 1 5
Did you notice that both hands
moved in the same direction?
We call this similar motion.
Practise this scale for next week.
Play it slowly so that the correct finger
falls on the correct note in each hand.

To finish this lesson we will look at **Follow the Leader**.
This way
FOLLOW the LEADER
Andante
1
5
f
5
1
Don't forget the finger changes!
1
5
3
4
3
5
4
p
f
5
1
3
2
3
1
2
Finger change in this hand as well!
Practise this piece for next time.
Now follow me to the next Worksheet!
It's not fair! Why can't I be the leader?
Stop moaning, Monty! – I'm trying to get to sleep!
Great! – I love doing the Worksheets!

# Worksheet 2

1
When both hands move in the same direction, it is called
..........................................
What is the meaning of the word **Andante**?
..........................................
What does this sign tell you to do?
When a dot is placed above or below a note, we play it
..........................................
Which scale have you learnt to play in **contrary motion**?
..........................................
..........................................
2
Write the letter names of the notes in the boxes.
3
Write these notes an octave lower in the bass clef.
4
Fill in the missing letters.
Q_ _ V_ _ _
C_ _ _ _ H_ _
_ _ N_ _
S_ _ _ B_ _ _ E

# Lesson 3

Let's begin with the scale exercise from Lesson 2.
Off we go – hands together!

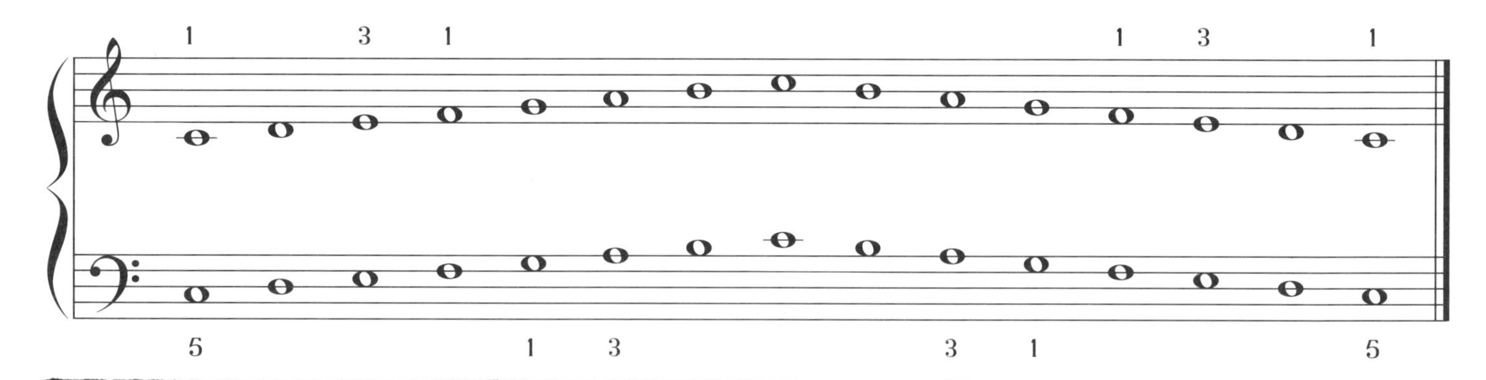


Play it once again for me.
Make sure that both hands play the notes together.
Remember to arch your fingers,
and do not drop your wrists.

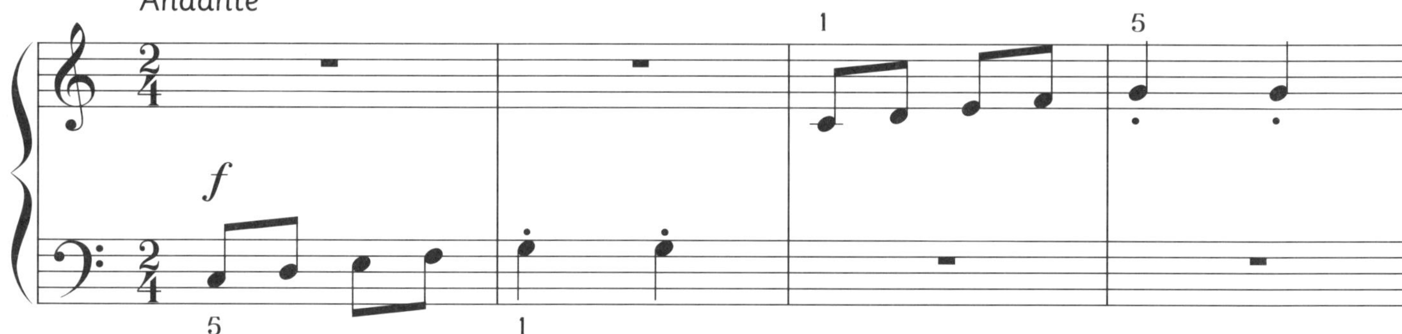


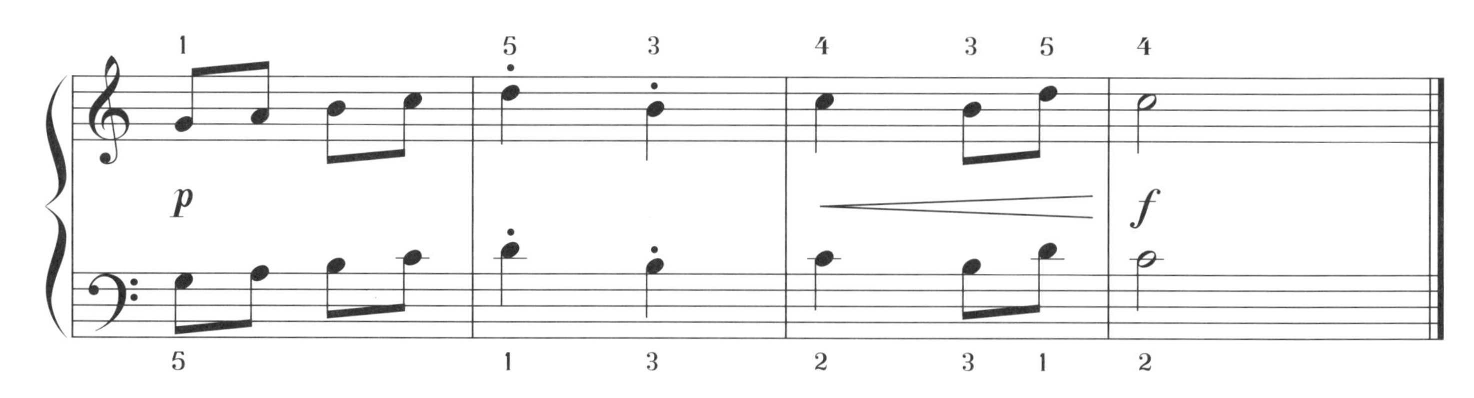

Do you remember this rhythm?
You learnt to play it in Book 2.
It sounds the same as this
Clap it for me.
Clap this next rhythm in 3/4 time.
Your teacher will clap with you.
Don't clap too loud!
It sounds the same as this.
This rhythm appears
in the next piece.
Turn over the page
and see if you can find it.

Clap the rhythm of your part with your teacher.

Take a careful look through this duet.
Look at each clef sign.
Both your hands are playing in the treble clef.

Do you see the instruction 8va
at the start of the piece?
This tells you to play your right hand part
eight notes (an octave) higher than written.

Practise it at home before your next lesson.
I look forward to hearing it with your teacher.

Don't forget! - this means play again from the beginning...
Will you let me get some sleep now?

Worksheet 3
1
How many notes are there in an octave?
What is the sign that tells you to play an octave higher?
2
Put barlines in the following to give the correct number of beats in each bar.
3
Correct the rhythm in each bar to give the right number of beats.

**4** Colour in the picture.

Lesson 4
We will start today's lesson with something new.
If you look at the next piece, you will see long curved lines above the music.
These are called **slurs** or **phrase marks**.
Phrases are like musical sentences – they tell you where to breathe in the music.
Let's play through this piece.
This is a phrase mark
SNAIL'S PACE
legato
p
pp
This means finish very quietly
Now play it again, taking care of the phrasing.
Will you practise this for me for next time?
Good!

**Slurring** notes together in the music gives expression, especially if you play the first note of each group a little firmer.
Look at this example.
The **phrase marks** show you which notes to slur. Drop onto the first note and gently bounce off the second.
Mi - aow, mi - aow, mi - aow, woof!
Hey!-that's **my** song!!
And now a three-note slur.
Let's finish this lesson by playing again the duet **Sailing in Space** from Lesson 3.

Worksheet 4
1
Name this symbol.
How should you play these notes?
And these ones? (Clue: Miaow)
2
Join each pair of crotchets with a slur.

3
Add a slur to the crotchets in each bar.
Add two phrase marks to the music.
4
Complete the dot-to-dot picture.
What piece does this remind you of?

Lesson 5
Let us begin our lesson with Snail's Pace.
legato
p
pp
And now for something different.
Look closely.
HOT NOTE HOE-DOWN
Moderato
p
f
ff
ff means 'very loudly'!
Oh, no!

Do you see that both hands play the same notes, but an octave apart?

Now play it.

Remember to keep your wrists loose and curve your fingers. All the notes should be played very short as they are marked **staccato**.

Play it once more.
Make sure you take notice of all the louds and softs – we call these **dynamics**.

And now for a new piece for you to learn and practise at home.

# FLYING HIGH

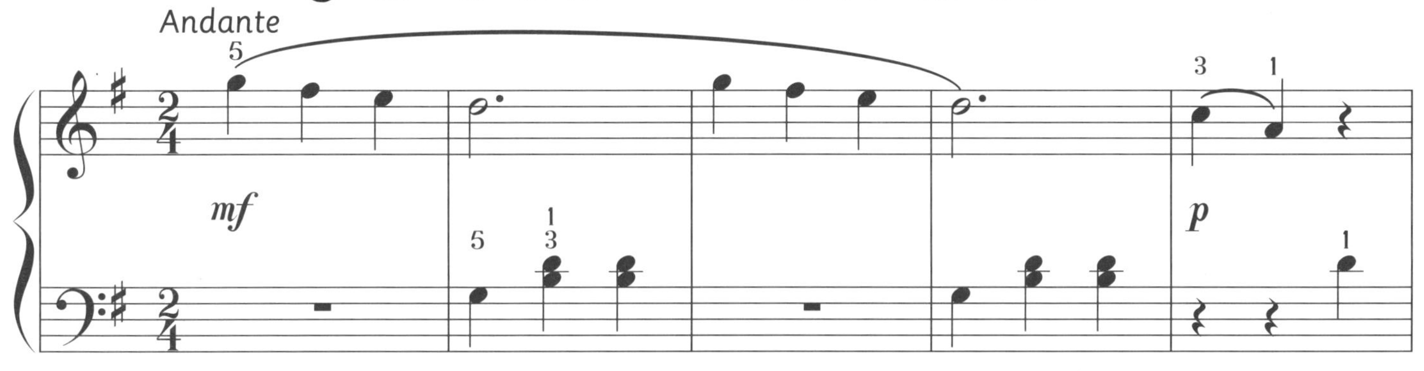


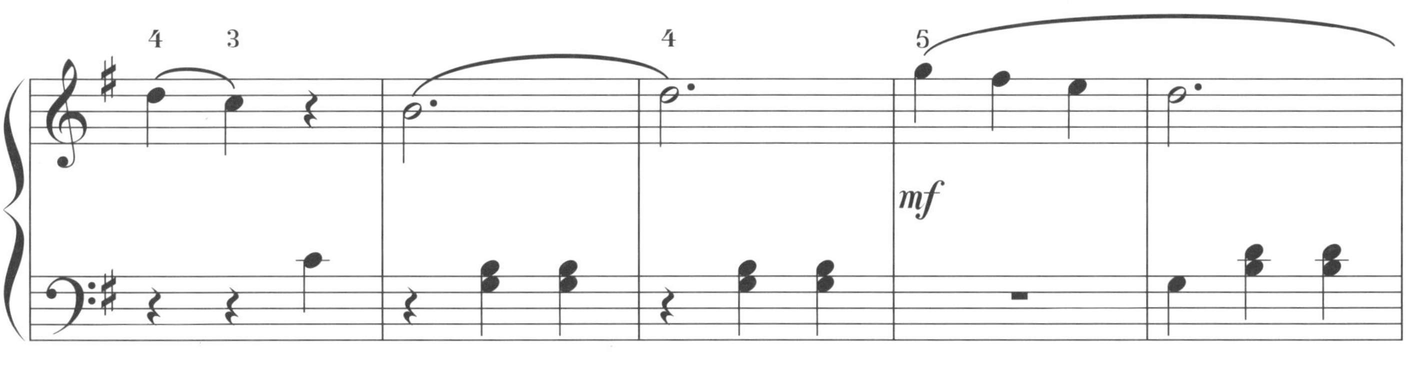


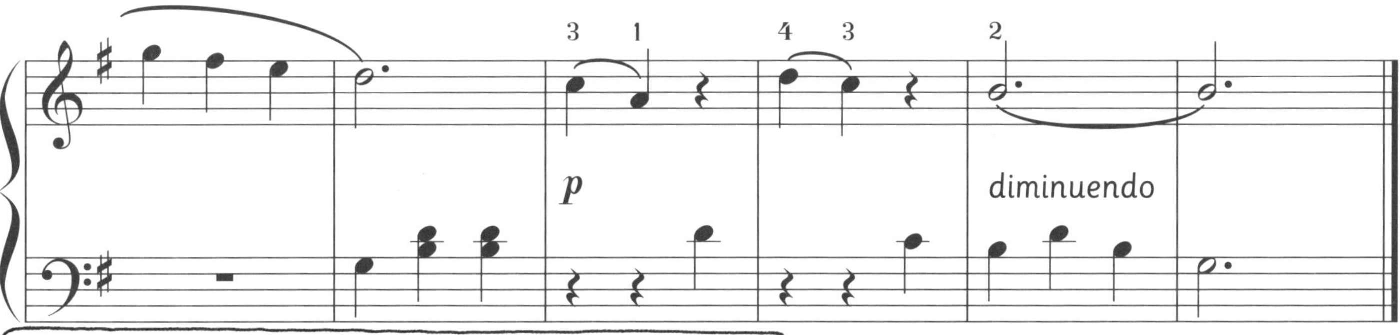


Do you want to try it through before we go?

# Worksheet 5

Do it quietly, please!

**Clues Across**

1. Which word describes getting quieter?
5. I can play my drum in a **b** _ _ _. (a group of musicians)
6. Speed in music is called **t** _ _ _ _.
7. What are four beat notes called?
8. Which word describes getting louder?
11. This sign $\frac{4}{4}$ is called a **t** _ _ _ signature.
13. What is the musical term for loud?

**Clues Down**

2. What is a two beat note called?
3. Does this note ♩ equal two beats?
4. When playing the piano, always keep an **e** _ _ on the music.
5. What is this sign called? 𝄢
6. $\frac{3}{4}$ means _ _ _ _ _ crotchet beats in a bar.
9. Take **c** _ _ _ to curve your fingers when playing the piano.
10. Middle C is a white **n** _ _ _.
12. What musical sign stands for moderately loud?

Today we are going to learn all about **semitones** and **whole tones**.

You already know that a **sharp** ♯ placed before a note tells you to play the black note above it. The distance between these two notes is called a **semitone**.

A **flat** ♭ before a note tells you to play the black note below it – a **semitone** below.

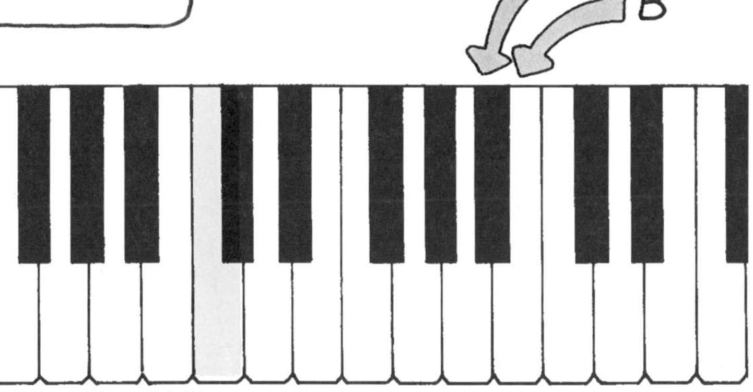


A semitone can also be between two white notes that are next to each other. Can you find some of these on the keyboard?

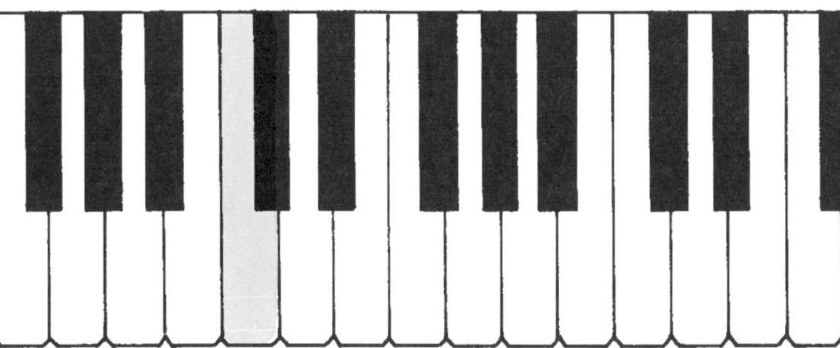

Yes, they are between E and F and B and C.

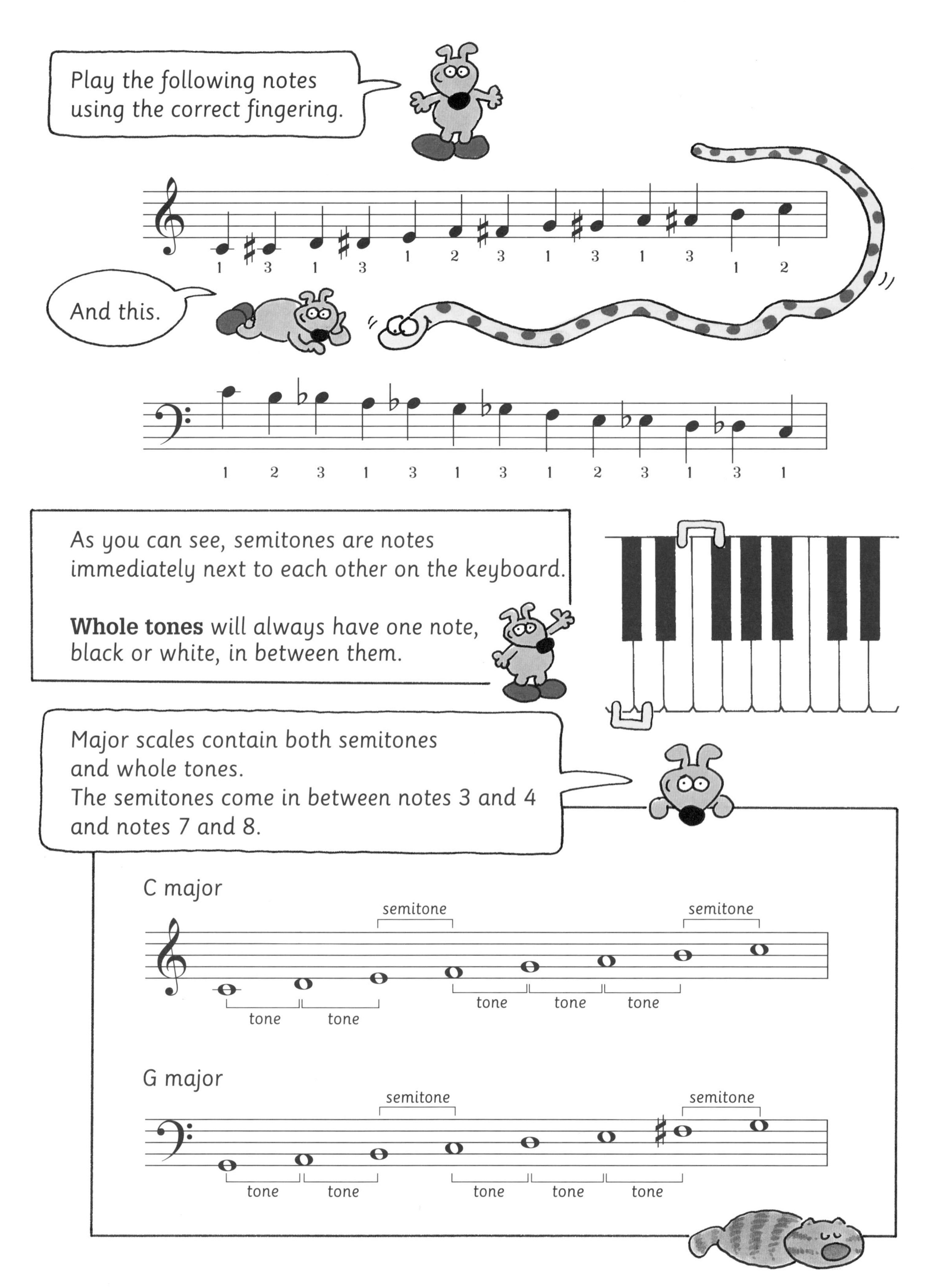
Play the following notes
using the correct fingering.
1 3 1 3 1 2 3 1 3 1 3 1 2
And this.
1 2 3 1 3 1 3 1 2 3 1 3 1
As you can see, semitones are notes
immediately next to each other on the keyboard.
**Whole tones** will always have one note,
black or white, in between them.
Major scales contain both semitones
and whole tones.
The semitones come in between notes 3 and 4
and notes 7 and 8.
C major
semitone
semitone
tone
tone
tone
tone
tone
G major
semitone
semitone
tone
tone
tone
tone
tone

Let's finish by playing **Flying High**.

# FLYING HIGH

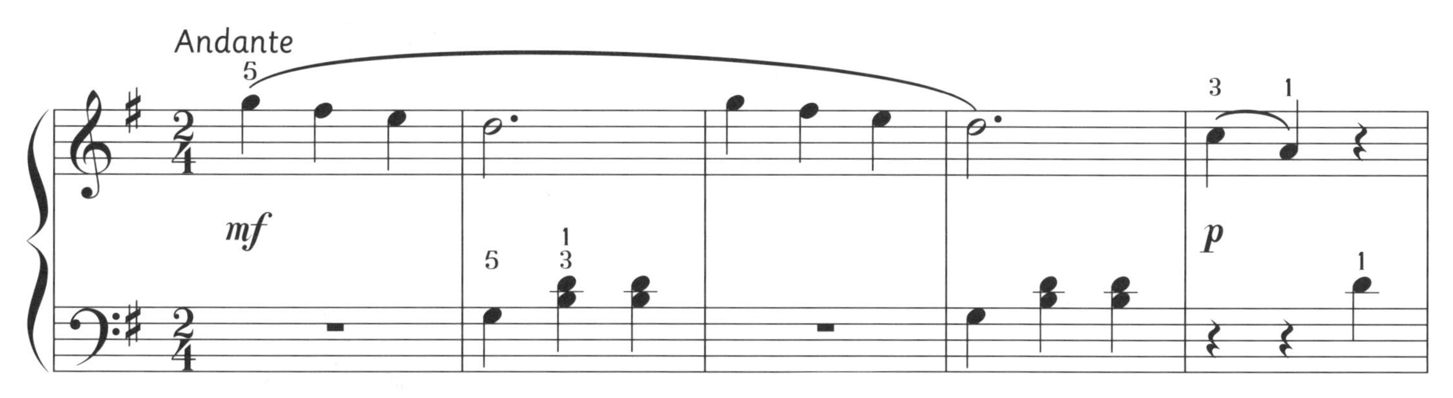


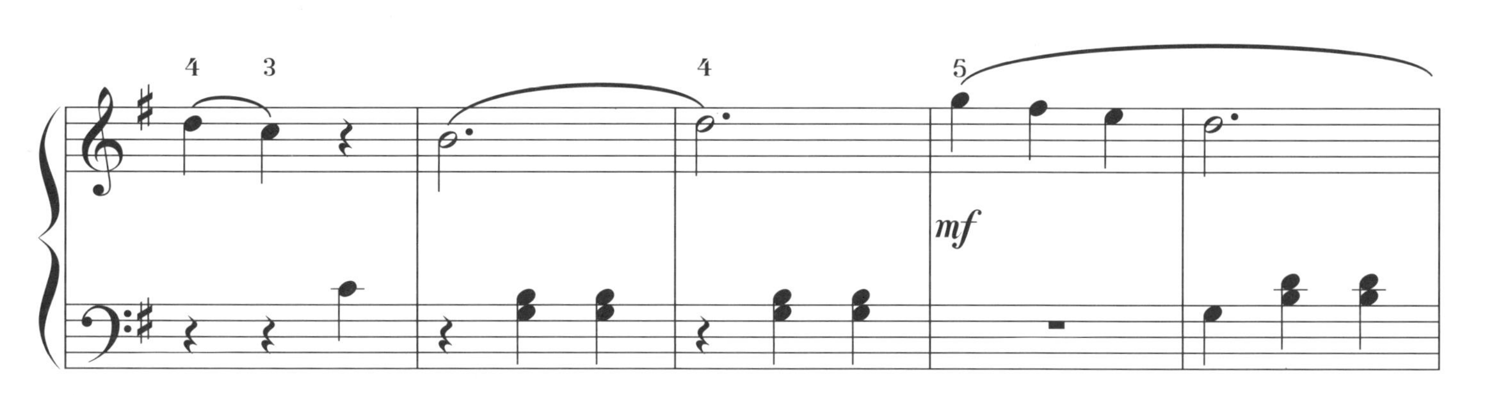


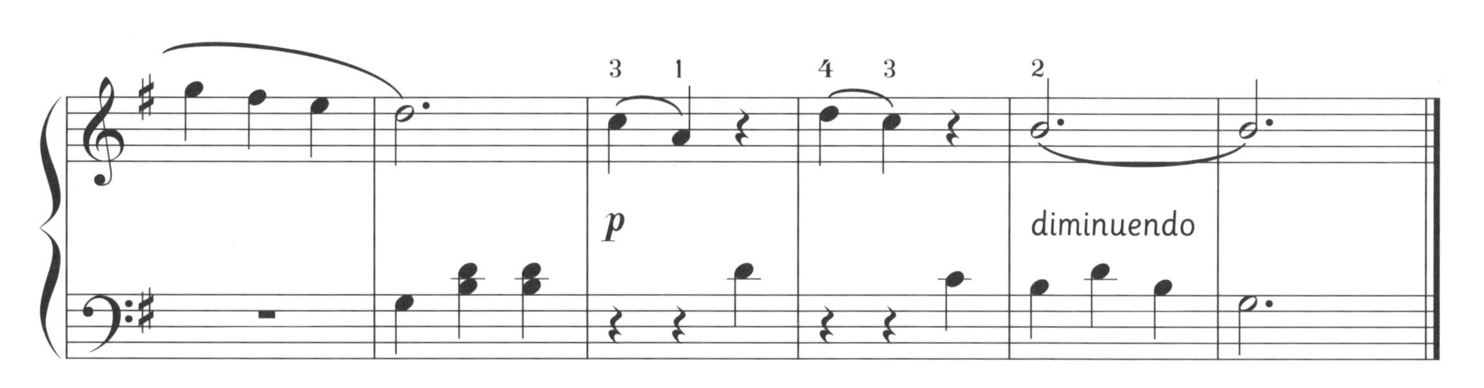


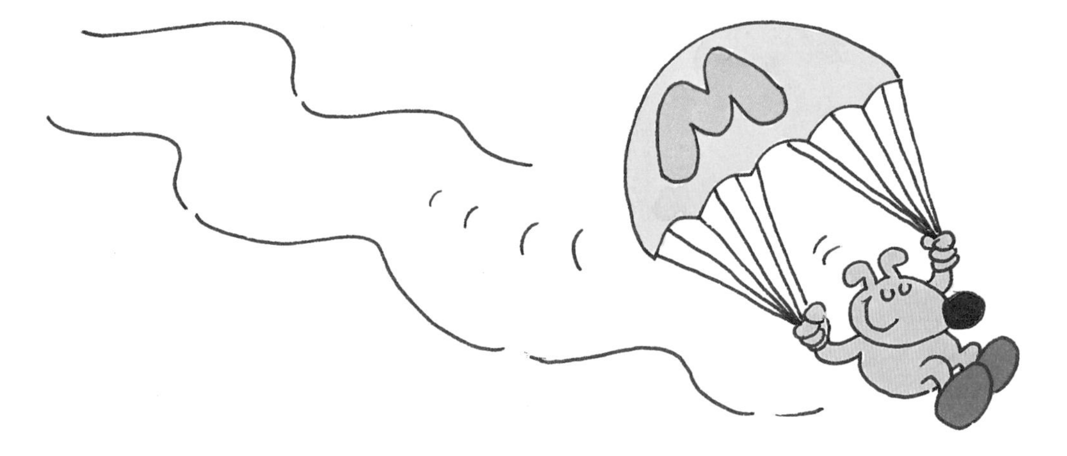

Worksheet 6
1
Write a sharp in front of the second note in each bar to make it a semitone higher.
2
Write a flat in front of the second note in each bar to make it a semitone lower.
3
Mark the notes that are a semitone apart, and then name the scale.
Scale of ___ major.
Scale of ___ major.

4 Colour in the picture.

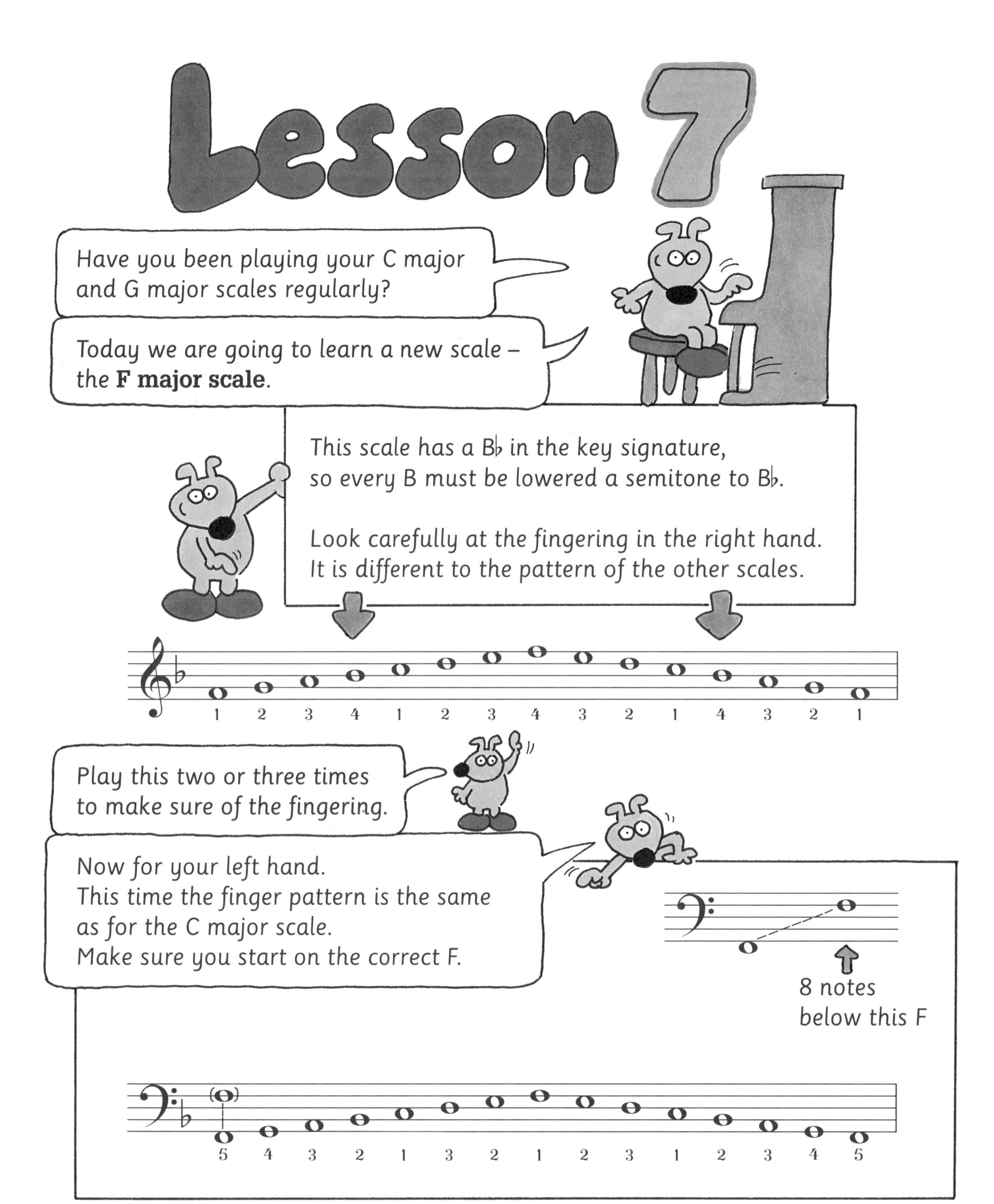


Practise this scale at home along with the others.

Here is a piece of music in F major
for you to prepare.
You can sing along as you play.

# COMPUTER SONG

# Worksheet 7

**1** Write in the missing key signatures.

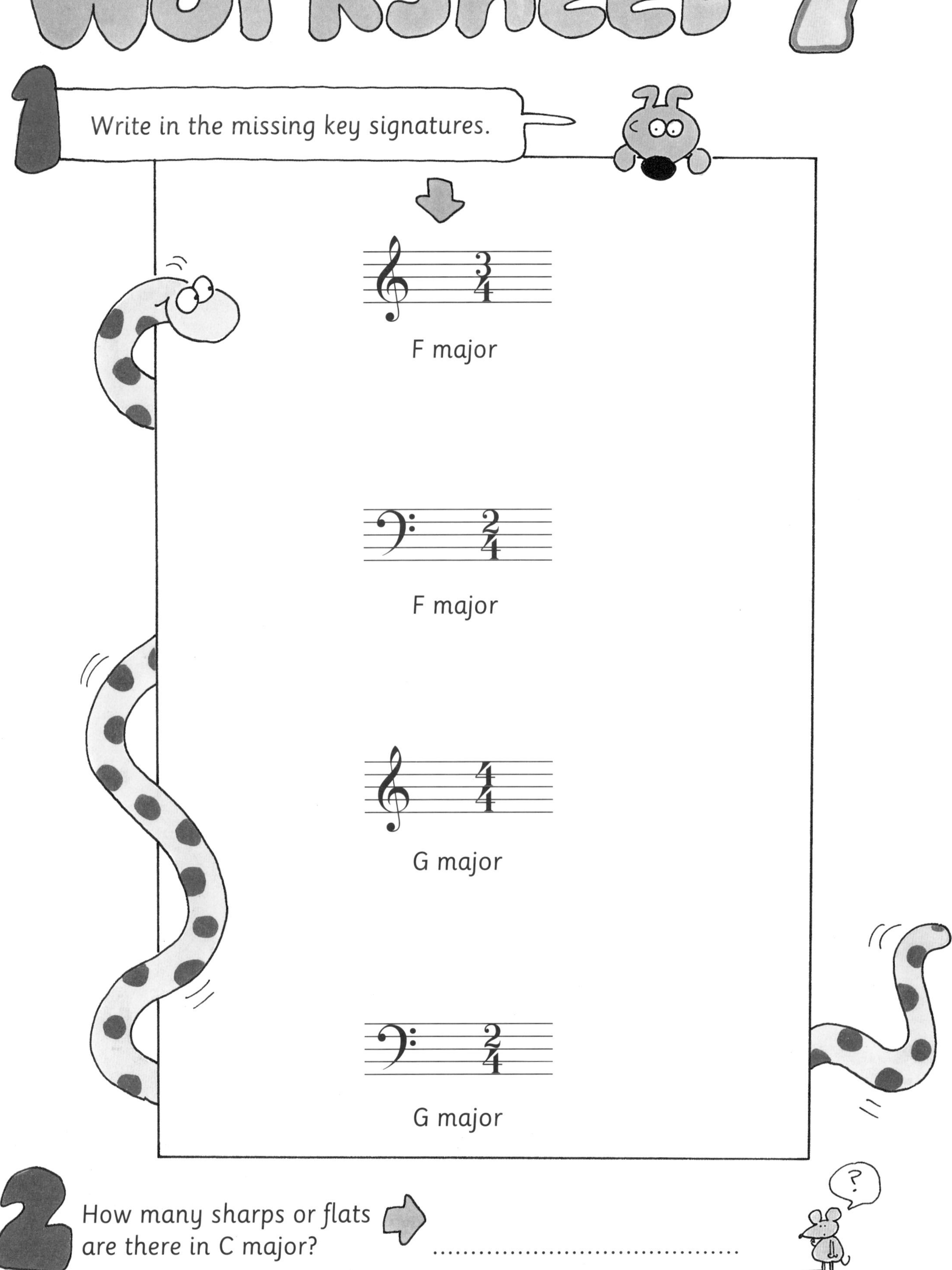


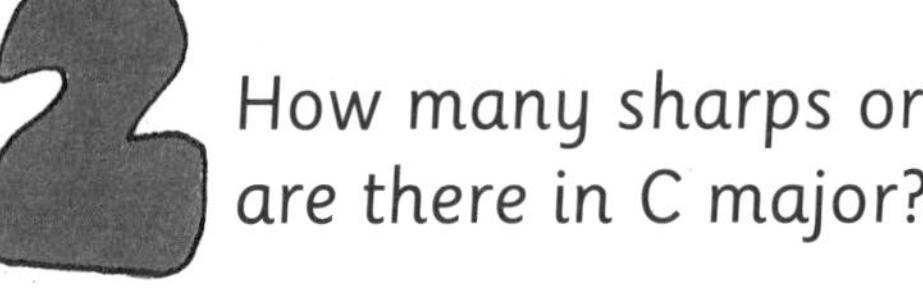

**2** How many sharps or flats are there in C major?  ........................................

Write out the scale of F major in crotchets, colouring each note with a different colour. Use as many as you can find.

For the right hand

For the left hand

Try and find the following words.

quietly!

| | | | |
|---|---|---|---|
| A TEMPO | DOTTED MINIM | QUAVER | SHARP |
| ALLEGRO | FLAT | RALL | SLUR |
| ANIMATO | MAX | REST | TIE |
| CRESCENDO | | | VIVO |

| | | | | | | | | | | | |
|---|---|---|---|---|---|---|---|---|---|---|---|
| T | A | L | F | H | E | Q | N | L | D | L | S |
| F | M | Q | V | T | U | A | U | S | T | X | H |
| O | A | N | I | M | A | T | O | A | A | I | A |
| D | X | J | V | I | T | E | K | L | V | J | R |
| N | U | Z | O | N | R | M | B | L | V | E | P |
| E | N | J | E | S | L | P | E | G | H | L | R |
| C | P | Q | T | O | M | O | D | W | B | U | P |
| S | G | S | U | V | C | R | A | L | L | O | F |
| E | E | O | M | A | N | W | M | S | U | T | Y |
| R | D | O | T | T | E | D | M | I | N | I | M |
| C | B | Y | A | L | L | E | G | R | O | E | R |

Solution on page 47

Today we are going to learn a new time signature.
But first, let's play **Computer Song**
from your last lesson.

And now for that new time signature.
$\frac{6}{8}$ tells you to count six quavers in each bar.

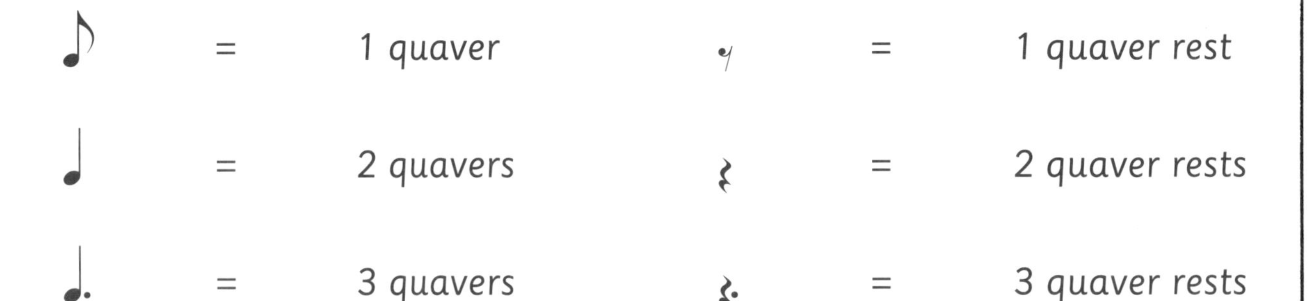

| | | | | | |
|---|---|---|---|---|---|
| ♪ | = | 1 quaver | 𝄾 | = | 1 quaver rest |
| ♩ | = | 2 quavers | 𝄽 | = | 2 quaver rests |
| ♩. | = | 3 quavers | 𝄽. | = | 3 quaver rests |
| 𝅗𝅥. | = | 6 quavers | | | |

Clap this rhythm with your teacher.
Make sure you count six quavers in each bar.

Help!
I can't clap!

sigh I wish
I could count...

Look at this next piece in $\frac{6}{8}$ time.
The left hand has chords with three notes to play.
Play these chords several times.

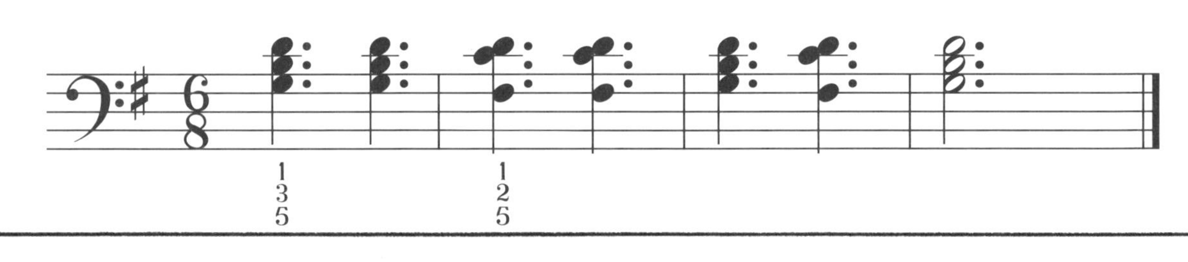

Now try the piece.
CLOWNING AROUND
Allegretto
mf
f
p
f
dim.
rit.
p
Practise this piece before your next lesson.
And don't forget to play your scales every day!

Worksheet 8
1
In 6/8 time, how many quavers do you count on each of these notes?
crotchet =
dotted crotchet =
dotted minim =
quaver =
2
In 6/8 time, how many quavers do you count on each of these rests?
I love rests!
=
=
3
Correct the rhythm by adding quaver tails or dots.
quaver tails look like this
4
Colour in this picture.

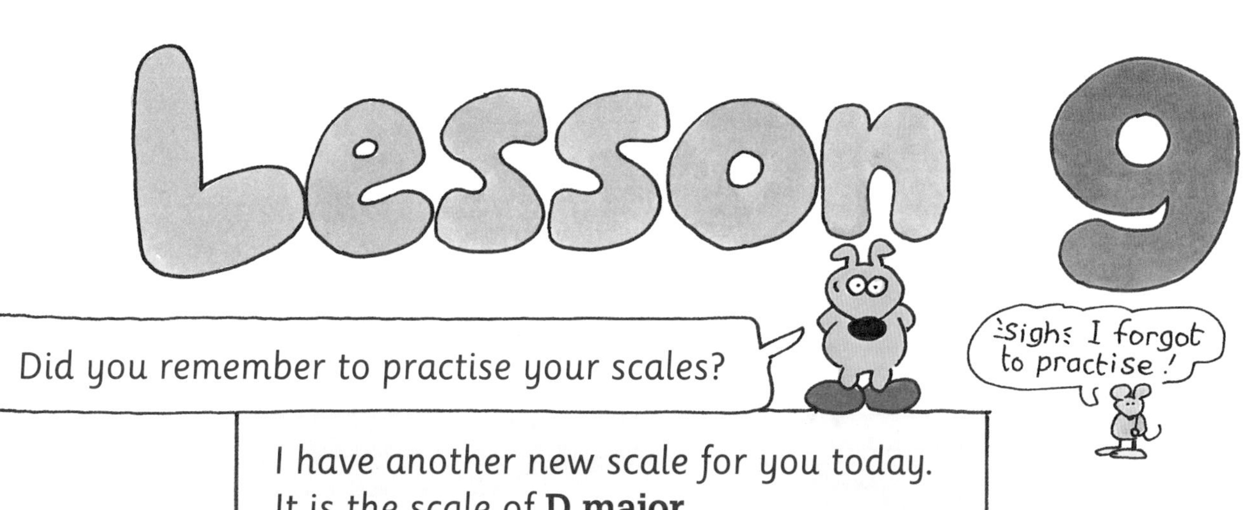
Lesson 9
Did you remember to practise your scales?
Sighs I forgot to practise!
I have another new scale for you today.
It is the scale of **D major.**

Can you see the two sharps in the key signature?
Yes, F sharp and C sharp.
1 2 3 1 2 3 4 5
Play this scale several times.
Don't forget the sharps!
You will remember that we don't have to write
the sharps in front of the note because
they are already in the key signature.
And now for the left hand.
5 4 3 2 1 3 2 1

Look carefully at the key signature of this next piece before you play it.
Watch out for the phrasing!
Hey! – this is my tune!
Sigh I wish I had my own tune!
Don't forget this!
SNAKE SKIN
Moderato

We will finish today by looking at another new piece.
Will you practise this for me for next time?
I hope it's my tune!

I like the sound of this one!

# TIME for BED

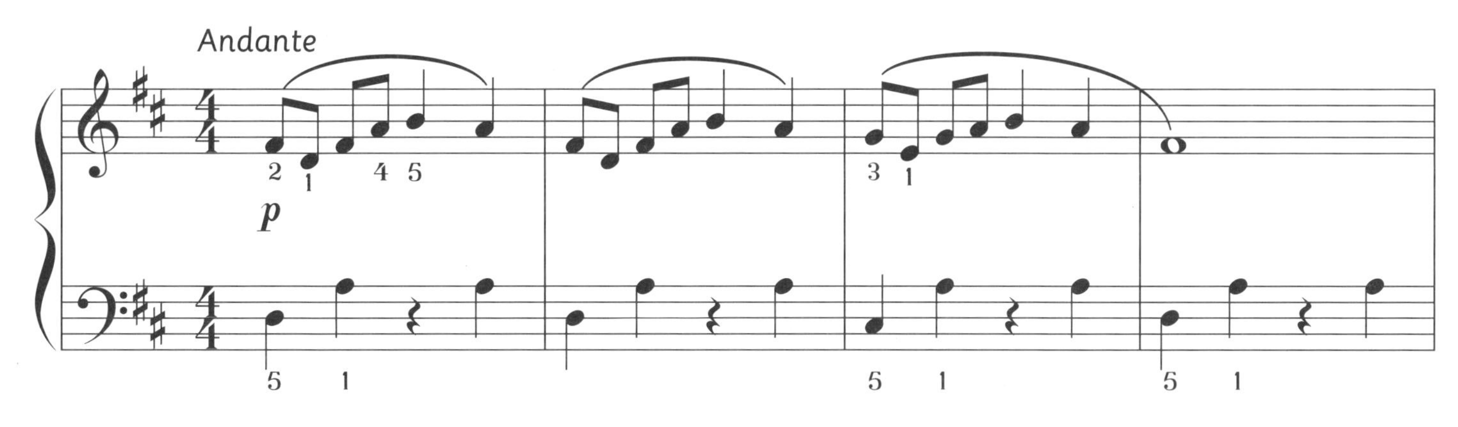

# Worksheet 9

**1** Write out the scale of D major in minims, then colour each of the sharp notes with a different colour.

**2** Name these keys, then write the first note of each scale as a semibreve.

**3** Is this scale in contrary motion or similar motion?

And this one?
4
Colour in this picture of Max.
MAXINE

Lesson 10
You have almost finished Book 3! Let's begin today's lesson by playing **Time for Bed**.
Well done!
TIME for BED
Andante
rall.
I hope you have been playing all the pieces in this book.
It is a good idea to play one or two of them at the end of your practise. When you have had some difficult things to sort out, you can finish by playing your favourite piece.
The next three pieces are for you to take home and learn. They include lots of the musical terms and new things that you have learnt.
Sigh I still can't reach the keys!

Oh, no – is it a loud one?
MAX WA-HEY
Allegro
mf
f
mf
f

# WALTZ in D

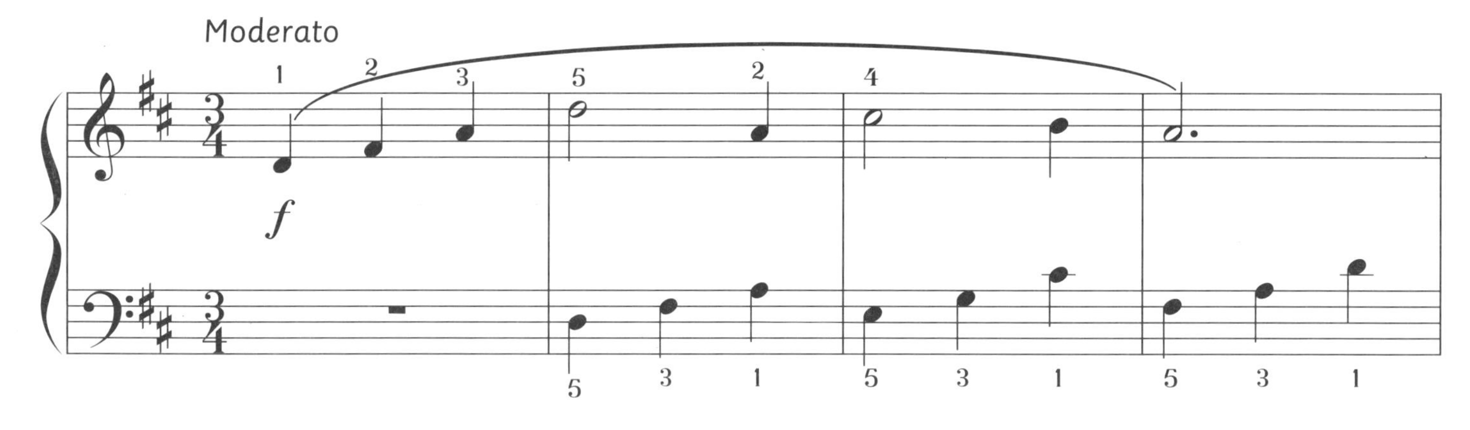


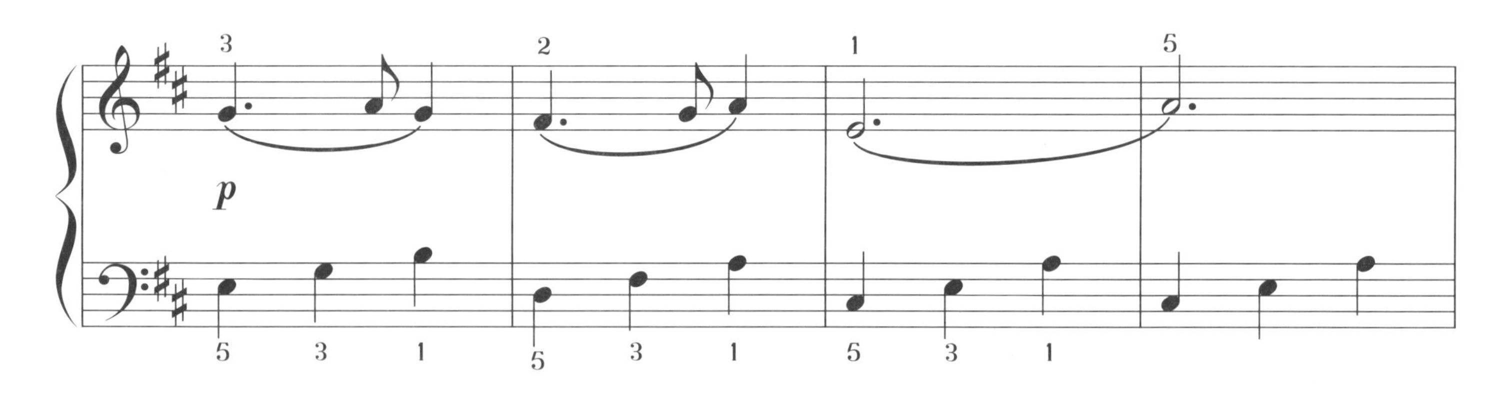

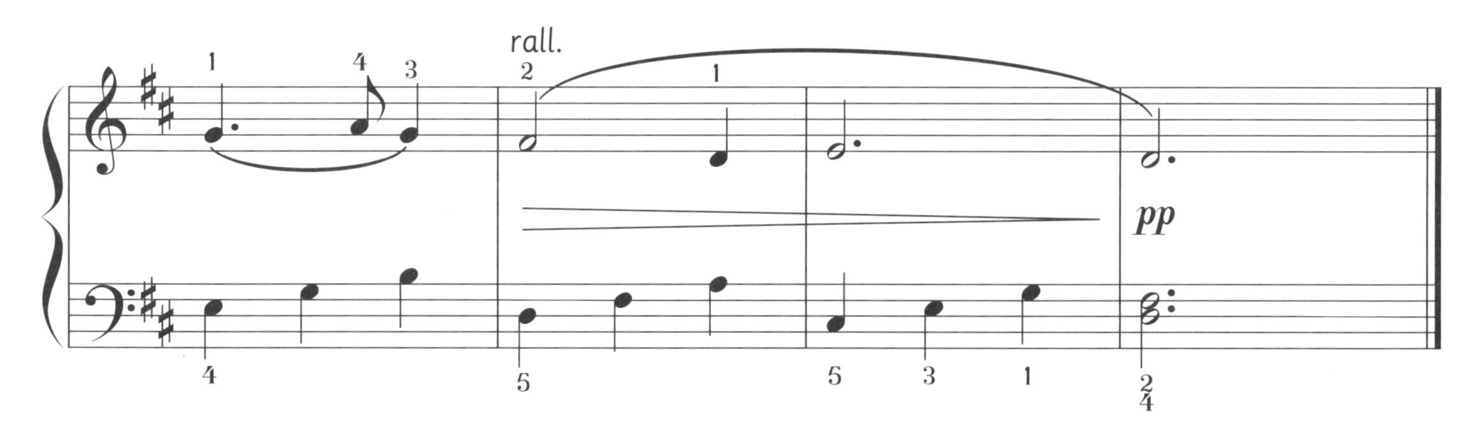

MONTY'S MELODY
Andante
mp
f
mp
p
rall.
pp
Repeat an octave higher
Hooray! At last! — this is my tune! It's the best one!
No, it's not! 'Snake Skin' is the best one!
Oh, no it isn't!! 'Time for Bed' is the best one!

I hope you enjoy playing these pieces.

There is no worksheet this time.
Instead there is a page to help you remember all the things you have learnt so far.

And don't forget –

- Practise the piano as much as you can – every day if possible.
- Make sure your stool or chair is at the right height, so that you can sit correctly.
- Always curve your fingers, and keep your hands and wrists in the right position.
- Always wash your hands before practising, and make sure you keep your fingernails short.

I'll always be around listening.

So will I!

Me, too!

– and I'll be around sleeping!

I think 'Max Wa-hey' is the best tune!

| | |
|---|---|
| > – | accent or stress mark – play more firmly |
| allegretto | fairly quickly, but not hurried |
| allegro | fast |
| andante | at a walking pace |
| animato | excitedly |
| a tempo | go back to the original speed |
| crescendo or cresc. | gradually getting louder |
| diminuendo or dim. | gradually getting quieter |
| forte *f* | loudly |
| fortissimo *ff* | very loud |
| legato | smoothly |
| 8va | play an octave higher |
| mezzo forte *mf* | moderately loud |
| mezzo piano *mp* | moderately soft |
| moderato | at a moderate speed |
| 𝄐 | pause mark – wait on the note a little longer |
| pianissimo *pp* | very quietly |
| piano *p* | quietly |
| poco a poco | little by little |
| rallentando or rall. | getting slower |
| ritenuto or rit. | slow down – hold back |
| staccato | short, detached notes |
| tempo | the speed or time to play a piece |
| vivo | lively |

Here is the solution to the wordsearch on page 33

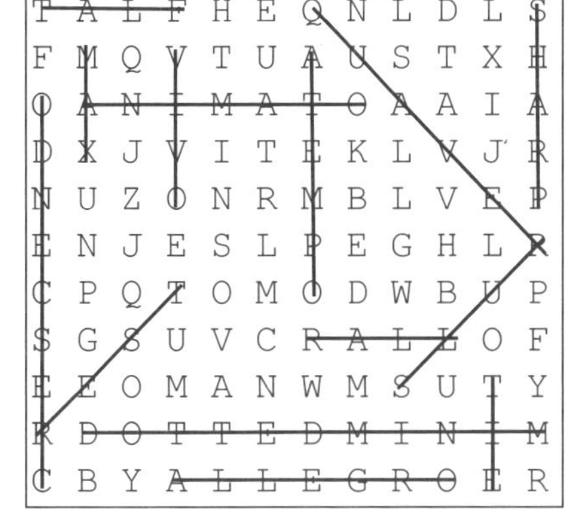

This is to certify that

........................................................................................................

has successfully completed

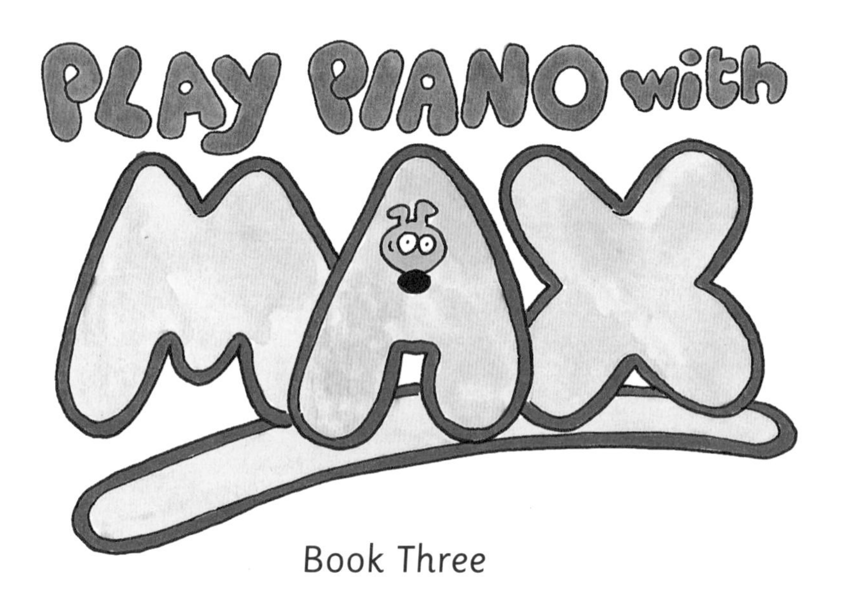


Book Three

Teacher ..........................................

Date ..........................................

Max

Myrna Stent

Myrna Stent